AM I OVERTHINKING

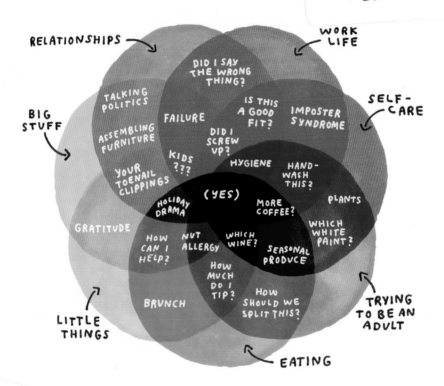

2022 Engagement Calendar
by Michelle Rial

CHRONICLE BOOKS

SAN FRANCISCO

ISBN: 978-1-7972-1064-3

FSC
www.fsc.org
MIX
Paper from
responsible sources
FSC™ C137129

Manufactured in China.

Chronicle Books LLC
680 Second Street
San Francisco, CA 94107
www.chroniclebooks.com

IS IT TOO LATE TO START?

PERCEPTION

BIRTH   DEATH

"TOO OLD"

↑
TOO
LATE
NOW

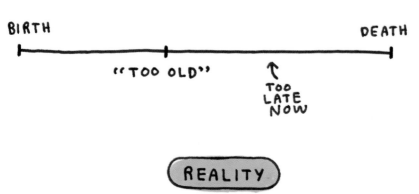

REALITY

BIRTH   DEATH

↑ STILL
GOOD

↑
TOO
LATE
NOW

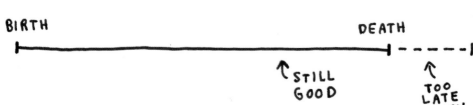

December/January

monday 27

tuesday 28

wednesday 29

thursday 30

friday 31 NEW YEAR'S EVE

saturday 1

NEW YEAR'S DAY

sunday 2

● NEW MOON

to-dos

IS THIS TOO LUXURIOUS?

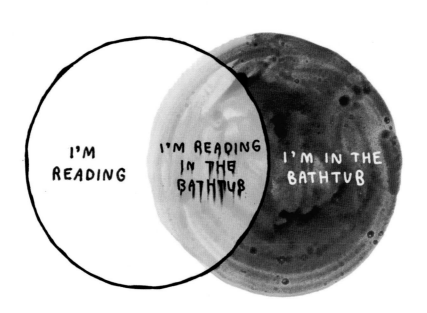

I'M READING

I'M READING IN THE BATHTUB

I'M IN THE BATHTUB

January

monday 3 BANK HOLIDAY (UK)

tuesday 4 BANK HOLIDAY (SCT)
WORLD BRAILLE DAY

wednesday 5

thursday 6 EPIPHANY

friday 7

saturday 8
NATIONAL BUBBLE BATH DAY

sunday 9
◗ FIRST QUARTER

to-dos

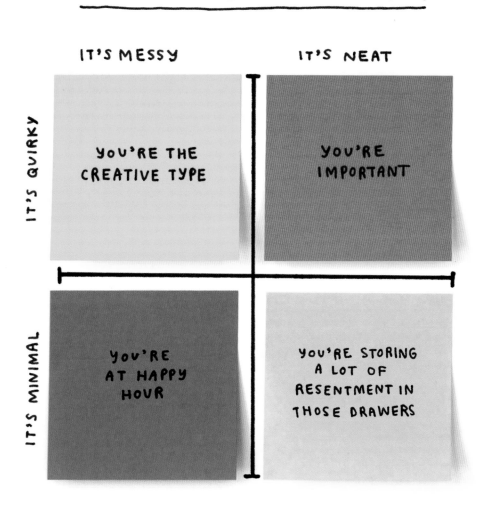

January

monday **10**	
tuesday **11**	
wednesday **12**	
thursday **13**	CLEAN OFF YOUR DESK DAY
friday **14**	

saturday **15**	sunday **16**

to-dos

WHAT IS THERE TO BE GRATEFUL FOR?

THERE'S ALWAYS SOMETHING						
LIFE	LIFE	LIFE	KETTLE CORN	LIFE	LIFE	SELTZER
LIFE	LIFE	LOVE	LIFE	LIFE	HEALTH	LIFE
WATER	LIFE	FAMILY	LIFE	MOVE-MENT	LIFE	THE WOODS
MUSIC	DANCE	LIFE	FRIENDS	HOT TEA	CLEAN AIR	A HOME
LAUGH-TER	THE SUN	LIFE				

January

monday **17** ○ FULL MOON
MARTIN LUTHER KING JR. DAY

tuesday **18**

wednesday **19** POPCORN DAY

thursday **20**

friday **21**

saturday **22**

sunday **23**

to-dos

CAN YOU HANDLE
MY HANG-UPS?

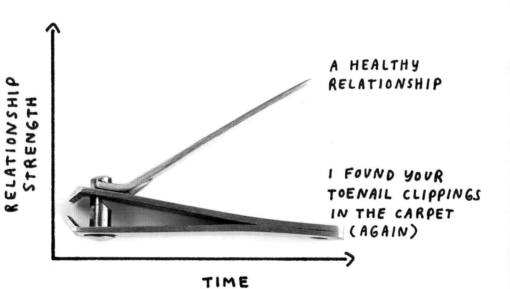

RELATIONSHIP
STRENGTH

A HEALTHY
RELATIONSHIP

I FOUND YOUR
TOENAIL CLIPPINGS
IN THE CARPET
(AGAIN)

TIME

January

monday **24**

tuesday **25**   ◑ LAST QUARTER

wednesday **26**   SPOUSE'S DAY

thursday **27**

friday **28**

saturday **29**

sunday **30**

to-dos

CAN I MAKE IT THROUGH
ANOTHER HARSH WINTER?

SELF-FULFILLMENT NEEDS
A HAT WITH A BALL ON IT

ESTEEM NEEDS
A WARM COAT THAT
LOOKS NICE

COZY NEEDS
MOODY MUSIC,
SOFT BLANKETS,
TWINKLE LIGHTS,
HOT CHOCOLATE,
HOT CIDER,
HOT TODDY

AFETY NEEDS
THE IDEAL
SEAT AT MY
FAVORITE CAFÉ

A HIERARCHY
OF WINTER COPING
MECHANISMS

January/February

monday 31

tuesday 1 ● NEW MOON
BLACK HISTORY MONTH BEGINS (US, CAN)
LUNAR NEW YEAR

wednesday 2 GROUNDHOG DAY

thursday 3

friday 4 WORLD CANCER DAY

saturday 5

sunday 6

to-dos

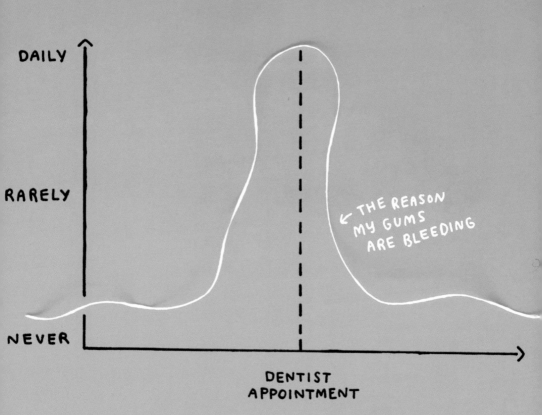

February

monday **7**

tuesday **8**   ◑ FIRST QUARTER

wednesday **9**   NATIONAL TOOTHACHE DAY

thursday **10**

friday **11**

saturday **12**

sunday **13**

to-dos

WHAT DOES THIS *mean* ?

THEY SAID...	IT MIGHT MEAN	BUT IT PROBABLY MEANS
THINGS ARE BUSY AT WORK	WORK IS SO BUSY RIGHT NOW	YOU'RE NOT A PRIORITY
I JUST GOT OUT OF A RELATIONSHIP	I'M READY FOR SOMETHING NEW	I STILL LOVE MY EX
I DON'T WANT TO PUT LABELS ON THIS	I'M EVOLVED AND MATURE	I'M KEEPING MY OPTIONS OPEN
MAYBE WE SHOULD PUT THIS ON PAUSE	I NEED A MOMENT TO REFLECT	
[NOTHING]	DIED ?	MY INTEREST IN YOU DIED ☹
MISS YOU	I WANT TO GET BACK TOGETHER	I SAW THAT YOU'RE HAPPY

February

monday 14 VALENTINE'S DAY

tuesday 15 SINGLES AWARENESS DAY

wednesday 16 ◯ FULL MOON

thursday 17

friday 18

saturday 19

sunday 20

WORLD DAY OF SOCIAL JUSTICE

to-dos

AM I GOOD AT MY JOB?

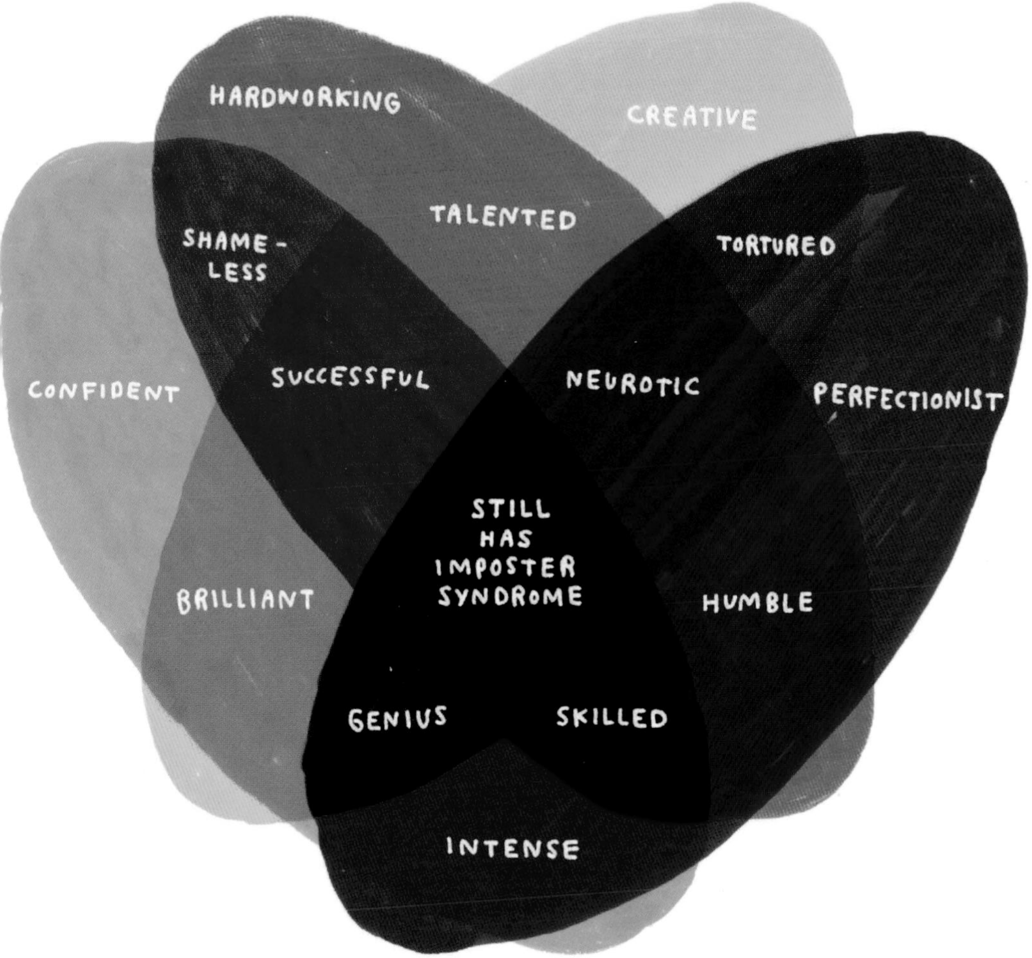

February

monday **21** PRESIDENTS' DAY (US)

tuesday **22** BE HUMBLE DAY

wednesday **23** ◐ LAST QUARTER

thursday **24**

friday **25**

saturday **26**

sunday **27**

to-dos

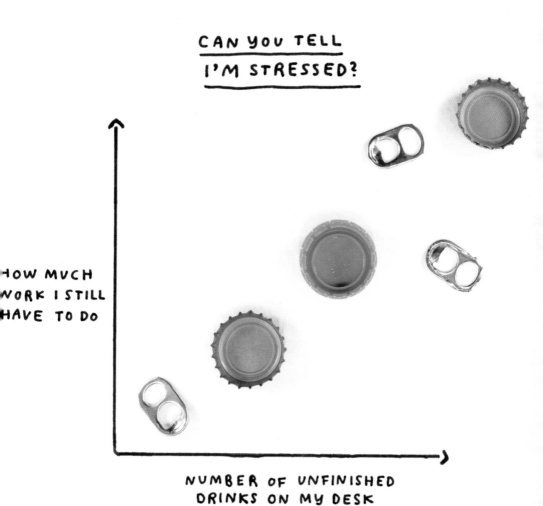

February/March

monday 28 MAHA SHIVARATRI

tuesday 1

wednesday 2 ● NEW MOON
ASH WEDNESDAY

thursday 3

friday 4 EMPLOYEE APPRECIATION DAY

saturday 5

sunday 6

to-dos

IS IT NORMAL TO CRY ON YOUR BIRTHDAY?

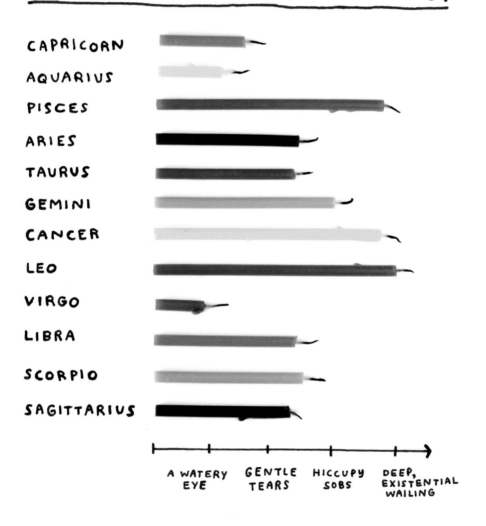

CAPRICORN

AQUARIUS

PISCES

ARIES

TAURUS

GEMINI

CANCER

LEO

VIRGO

LIBRA

SCORPIO

SAGITTARIUS

A WATERY   GENTLE   HICCUPY   DEEP,
EYE   TEARS   SOBS   EXISTENTIAL
                                              WAILING

March

monday **7**

tuesday **8** INTERNATIONAL WOMEN'S DAY

wednesday **9**

thursday **10** ◗ FIRST QUARTER

friday **11**

saturday **12**

sunday **13**

DAYLIGHT SAVING TIME BEGINS (US, CAN)

to-dos

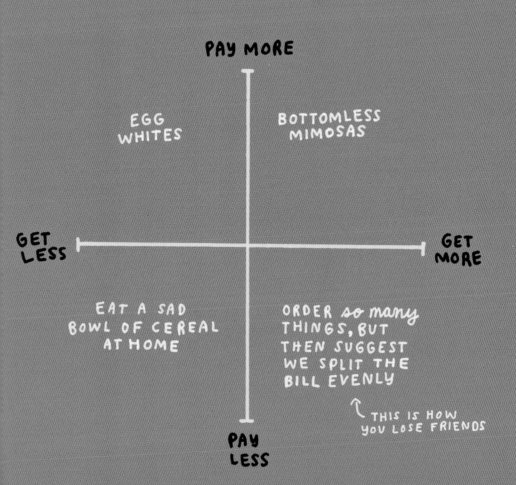

March

monday 14 NATIONAL BRUNCH DAY (US)

tuesday 15

wednesday 16 PURIM BEGINS

thursday 17 HOLI BEGINS
ST. PATRICK'S DAY

friday 18 ◯ FULL MOON

saturday 19

sunday 20

SPRING EQUINOX

to-dos

WILL PARENTHOOD
CHANGE EVERYTHING?

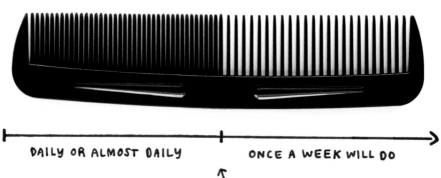

DAILY OR ALMOST DAILY   ONCE A WEEK WILL DO

↑ PARENTHOOD
BEGINS

(HAIR WASHING FREQUENCY)

March

monday	**21**	INTERNATIONAL DAY FOR THE ELIMINATION OF RACIAL DISCRIMINATION NOWRUZ BEGINS WORLD DOWN SYNDROME DAY NATIONAL SINGLE PARENTS DAY

tuesday **22**

wednesday **23**

thursday **24**

friday **25** ◗ LAST QUARTER

saturday **26**

sunday **27**

MOTHERING SUNDAY (UK, IRL)
SUMMER TIME BEGINS (UK, IRL)

to-dos

_____
_____
_____
_____
_____
_____
_____
_____
_____
_____
_____
_____
_____
_____
_____
_____
_____
_____
_____
_____

SHOULD I EAT THE REST OR SAVE IT ?

IF I SAVE HALF,
I'LL HAVE A
WHOLE MEAL
FOR LATER

JUST A FEW
MORE BITES

FORGET IT

March/April

monday **28**

tuesday **29**

wednesday **30**

thursday **31**   INTERNATIONAL TRANSGENDER
DAY OF VISIBILITY

friday **1**   ● NEW MOON

saturday **2**

RAMADAN BEGINS
WORLD AUTISM AWARENESS DAY
NATIONAL BURRITO DAY

sunday **3**

to-dos

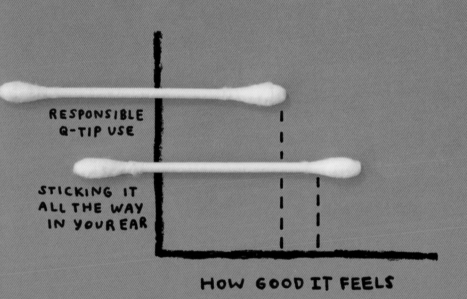

CAN I INJURE MYSELF
WHILE Q-TIPPING?

RESPONSIBLE
Q-TIP USE

STICKING IT
ALL THE WAY
IN YOUR EAR

HOW GOOD IT FEELS

April

monday **4**

tuesday **5** QINGMING FESTIVAL

wednesday **6**

thursday **7**

friday **8** VESAK

saturday **9**
● FIRST QUARTER

sunday **10**
PALM SUNDAY
Q-TIP'S BIRTHDAY

to-dos

AM I EATING
TOO MUCH CHEESE?

I HAVE
A HEALTHY
RELATIONSHIP
WITH CHEESE

I HAVE A
PROBLEM

GIVING UP
CHEESE
WOULD BE
A BRIE-ZE

I'M A
SOCIAL
EATER

ALL FOOD
IS A VEHICLE
FOR CHEESE

I'M
VERY
SICK

April

monday 11

tuesday 12 NATIONAL GRILLED CHEESE SANDWICH DAY

wednesday 13

thursday 14 SOLAR NEW YEAR

friday 15 GOOD FRIDAY
PASSOVER BEGINS

saturday 16
○ FULL MOON

sunday 17
EASTER

to-dos

WHAT IF IT'S TOO LATE?

DO

DON'T

↑
WORK
TOGETHER
TO MAKE
CHANGE

↑
BECOME
PARALYZED
BY DESPAIR

April

monday **18** EASTER MONDAY (CAN, UK, IRL)

tuesday **19**

wednesday **20**

thursday **21**

friday **22** EARTH DAY

saturday **23**

◑ LAST QUARTER
ST. GEORGE'S DAY (UK, IRL)

sunday **24**

ORTHODOX EASTER

to-dos

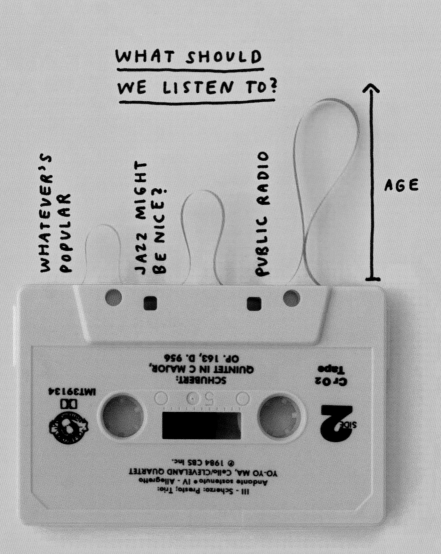

April/May

monday **25**

tuesday **26**

wednesday **27**   YOM HASHOAH BEGINS

thursday **28**

friday **29**

saturday **30**

● NEW MOON
INTERNATIONAL JAZZ DAY

sunday **1**

MAY DAY

to-dos

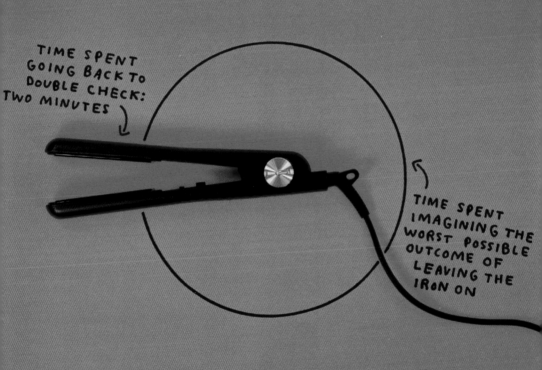

May

monday **2**

BANK HOLIDAY (UK, IRL)
EID AL-FITR BEGINS
NATIONAL CURLY HAIR DAY

tuesday **3**

wednesday **4**

thursday **5**

DÍA DE LA BATALLA DE PUEBLA

friday **6**

saturday **7**

sunday **8**

MOTHER'S DAY (US, CAN)

to-dos

WHY DON'T I BIKE
MORE OFTEN?

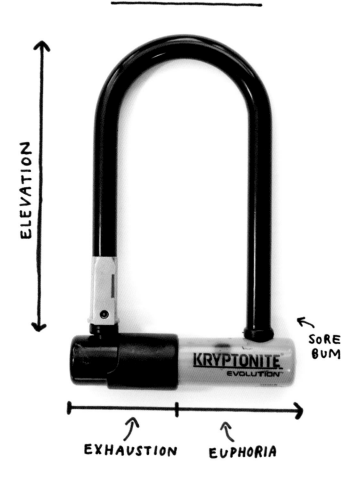

ELEVATION

SORE BUM

EXHAUSTION

EUPHORIA

May

monday **9** ◑ FIRST QUARTER

tuesday **10**

wednesday **11**

thursday **12**

friday **13**

saturday **14**

sunday **15**

BIKE TO WORK DAY

HOW LONG SHOULD
THIS DISH SOAK?

TOTAL
SOAKING
TIME

Ⓐ NECESSARY
SOAKING TIME

Ⓑ OOPS, I FORGOT
ABOUT IT

May

monday 16 ○ FULL MOON

tuesday 17 INTERNATIONAL DAY AGAINST HOMOPHOBIA, TRANSPHOBIA, AND BIPHOBIA

wednesday 18 NATIONAL NO DIRTY DISHES DAY

thursday 19

friday 20

saturday 21

sunday 22 ◑ LAST QUARTER

to-dos

IS IT WEDDING SEASON ALREADY?

TRIPS TO THE DRY CLEANER

J F M A M J J A S O N D

MONTH

May

monday **23** VICTORIA DAY (CAN)

tuesday **24**

wednesday **25**

thursday **26**

friday **27**

saturday **28**

sunday **29**

to-dos

STILL OR SPARKLING?

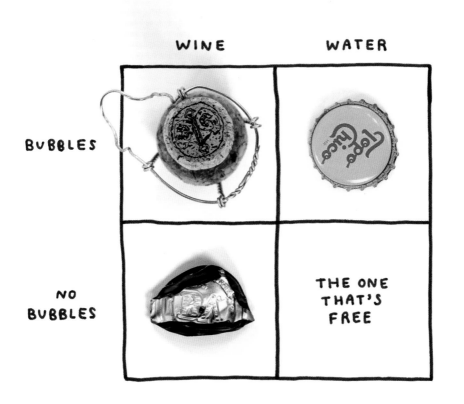

WINE   WATER

BUBBLES

NO
BUBBLES

THE ONE
THAT'S
FREE

May/June

monday 30 ● NEW MOON
MEMORIAL DAY OBSERVED (US)

tuesday 31

wednesday 1 PRIDE MONTH BEGINS (US)

thursday 2 BANK HOLIDAY (UK)

friday 3 DRAGON BOAT FESTIVAL
PLATINUM JUBILEE BANK HOLIDAY (UK)

saturday 4
NATIONAL BUBBLY DAY

sunday 5

to-dos

_____
_____
_____
_____
_____
_____
_____
_____
_____
_____
_____
_____
_____
_____
_____
_____
_____
_____
_____
_____
_____
_____
_____

WHAT'S SO GREAT
ABOUT CAMPING?

BUILDING A FIRE

S'MORES

S'MORES

WAKING UP FOR SUNRISE

THE STARS

THE STARS

S'MORES

NATURE SMELLS

NATURE SOUNDS

NATURE SMELLS

NATURE SMELLS

SETTING UP A TENT

SETTING UP A TENT

SLEEPING ON
THE GROUND

June

monday 6   BANK HOLIDAY (IRL)

tuesday 7   ◑ FIRST QUARTER

wednesday 8

thursday 9

friday 10

saturday 11

NATIONAL GET OUTDOORS DAY

sunday 12

to-dos

AM I DOING
ENOUGH?

June

monday **13**

tuesday **14** ○ FULL MOON
FLAG DAY (US)

wednesday **15**

thursday **16**

friday **17**

saturday **18**

sunday **19**

FATHER'S DAY (US, CAN, UK)
JUNETEENTH (US)

to-dos

WHAT CAN I LEARN
FROM THE OUTDOORS?

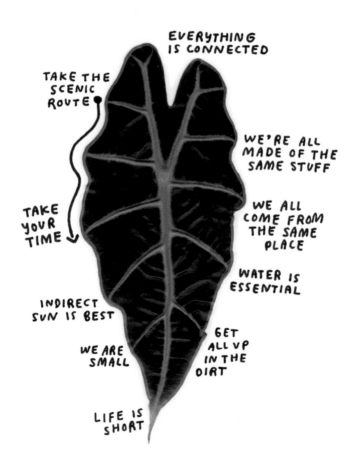

June

monday 20 WORLD REFUGEE DAY

tuesday 21 ◑ LAST QUARTER
SUMMER SOLSTICE
NATIONAL INDIGENOUS PEOPLES' DAY (CAN)

wednesday 22

thursday 23

friday 24

saturday 25

sunday 26

to-dos

HAS ANYONE SEEN MY SUNGLASSES?

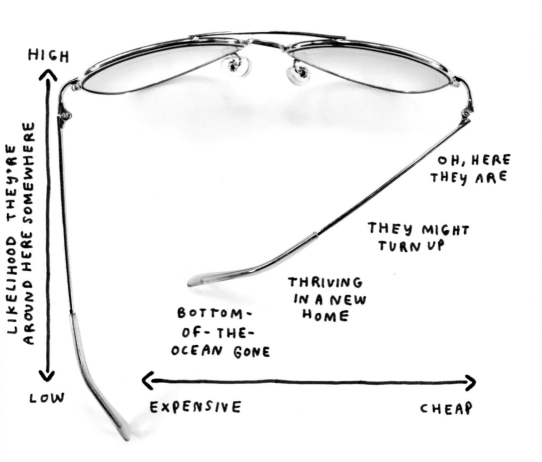

LIKELIHOOD THEY'RE AROUND HERE SOMEWHERE

HIGH

LOW

EXPENSIVE

CHEAP

OH, HERE THEY ARE

THEY MIGHT TURN UP

THRIVING IN A NEW HOME

BOTTOM-OF-THE-OCEAN GONE

June/July

monday 27 NATIONAL SUNGLASSES DAY

tuesday 28

wednesday 29 ● NEW MOON

thursday 30

friday 1 CANADA DAY (CAN)

saturday 2

sunday 3

to-dos

WHAT CAN I SERVE
AT THIS PARTY?

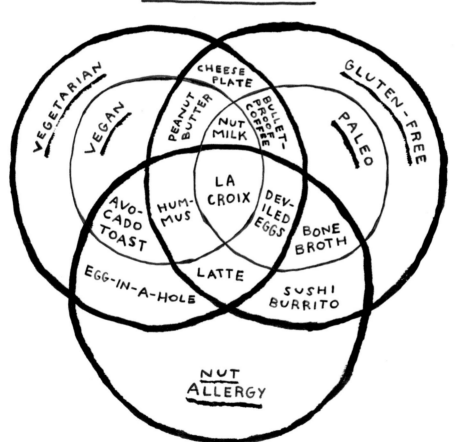

July

monday 4 INDEPENDENCE DAY (US)

tuesday 5

wednesday 6

thursday 7 ◗ FIRST QUARTER

friday 8

saturday 9

EID AL-ADHA BEGINS

sunday 10

to-dos

July

monday **11**

tuesday **12**   I FORGOT DAY

wednesday **13**   ◯ FULL MOON

thursday **14**

friday **15**

saturday **16**

sunday **17**

to-dos

SHOULD WE GET ICE CREAM?

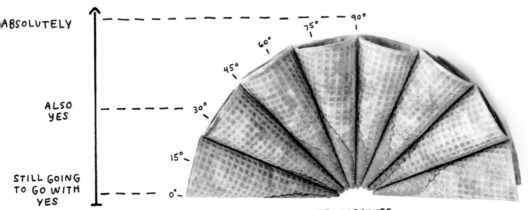

ABSOLUTELY

ALSO
YES

STILL GOING
TO GO WITH
YES

90°
75°
60°
45°
30°
15°
0°

LIKELIHOOD OF
ICE CREAM RUN

TEMPERATURE
IN FAHRENHEIT

July

monday **18**

tuesday **19**

wednesday **20** ◑ LAST QUARTER

thursday **21**

friday **22**

saturday **23**

sunday **24**

to-dos

WHICH F·R·I·E·N·D AM I?

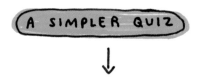

PICK A VOCAL FREQUENCY
THAT RESONATES WITH YOU

IF YOU HAVE A PROBLEM WITH THE LEVEL OF
SCIENTIFIC ACCURACY OF THIS QUIZ, YOU'RE ROSS

July

monday **25**

tuesday **26**

wednesday **27**

thursday **28** ● NEW MOON

friday **29**

saturday **30**

INTERNATIONAL DAY OF FRIENDSHIP

sunday **31**

to-dos

IS IT WATERMELON SEASON?

NORTHERN HEMISPHERE

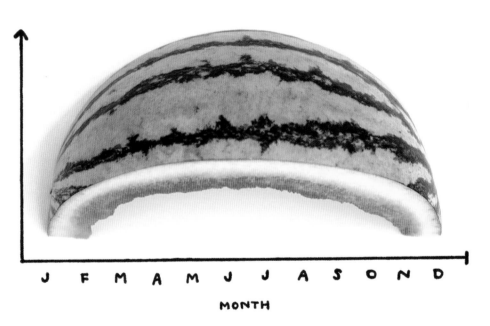

WATERMELON POPULARITY

J F M A M J J A S O N D

MONTH

August

monday **1** BANK HOLIDAY (SCT, IRL)

tuesday **2**

wednesday **3** NATIONAL WATERMELON DAY

thursday **4**

friday **5** ◗ FIRST QUARTER

saturday **6**

sunday **7**

ASHURA BEGINS

to-dos

SHOULD I LEND YOU MY BOOKS?

LIKELIHOOD I'LL LEND YOU MY FAVORITE BOOK

← I CAN'T STAND THE IDEA THAT YOU HAVEN'T READ IT

← YOU USE A BOOKMARK

← YOU'RE A DOG-EAR-ER

← I'VE SEEN YOU USE A BOOK AS A COASTER

← YOU READ IN THE BATHTUB

RISK

"He's trying to write
writing love stories. Bad
he'd let me. He writes th
just tell."

"Bad?"

"Substanceless."

"He's never been in l

"Probably not. Have
She nodded. She still

"Scrap thinks it mus
the stories."

"It is."

"I think it sounds nice."

"No." A thought edged its way out of her mouth. "You're substanceless, a little, I think."

August

monday **8**

tuesday **9**   INTERNATIONAL DAY OF THE WORLD'S
INDIGENOUS PEOPLE
BOOK LOVER'S DAY

wednesday **10**

thursday **11**

friday **12**   ◯ FULL MOON

saturday **13**

OBON BEGINS

sunday **14**

to-dos

SHOULD I GET RID OF THIS?

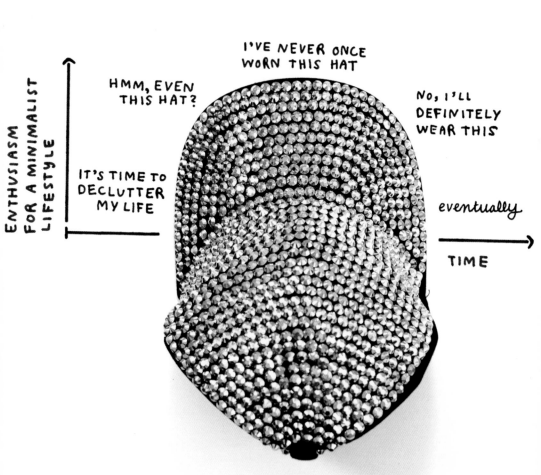

ENTHUSIASM FOR A MINIMALIST LIFESTYLE

HMM, EVEN THIS HAT?

IT'S TIME TO DECLUTTER MY LIFE

I'VE NEVER ONCE WORN THIS HAT

NO, I'LL DEFINITELY WEAR THIS

eventually

TIME

August

monday **15**

tuesday **16**

wednesday **17** THRIFT SHOP DAY

thursday **18**

friday **19** ◐ LAST QUARTER

saturday **20**

sunday **21**

to-dos

IS THIS WINE OK?

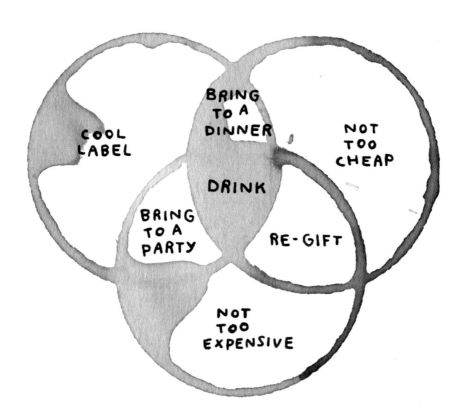

August

monday **22**

tuesday **23**

wednesday **24**

thursday **25**

friday **26**

saturday **27**

● NEW MOON

sunday **28**

NATIONAL RED WINE DAY

to-dos

WHAT DOES MY TOTE BAG SAY ABOUT ME?

I WANT YOU TO KNOW WHAT I CARE ABOUT

I CARE ABOUT REDUCING WASTE

I CARE ABOUT INDEPENDENT BOOKSTORES (ESPECIALLY IF THE LOGO IS NICE)

August/September

monday **29**   BANK HOLIDAY (ENG, N.IRL, WAL)
INDEPENDENT BOOKSTORE DAY

tuesday **30**

wednesday **31**

thursday **1**

friday **2**

saturday **3**
◑ FIRST QUARTER

sunday **4**

to-dos

_____
_____
_____
_____
_____
_____
_____
_____
_____
_____
_____
_____
_____
_____
_____
_____
_____
_____
_____
_____
_____
_____
_____

WHY DO I FEEL TERRIBLE?

September

monday 5   LABOR DAY (US, CAN)
NATIONAL CHEESE PIZZA DAY

tuesday 6

wednesday 7

thursday 8

friday 9

saturday 10

○ FULL MOON
MID-AUTUMN FESTIVAL
WORLD SUICIDE PREVENTION DAY

sunday 11

to-dos

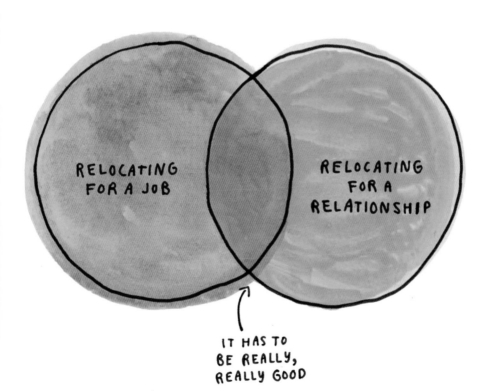

September

monday **12**

tuesday **13**

wednesday **14**

thursday **15**

friday **16**

saturday **17**
◖ LAST QUARTER

sunday **18**
NATIONAL FIRST LOVE DAY

to-dos

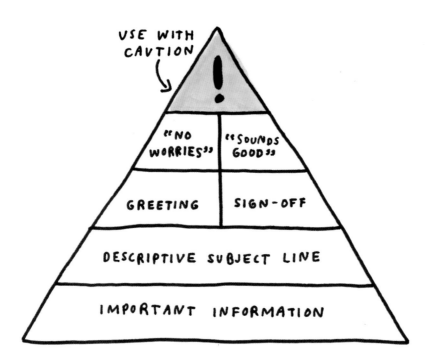

DOES THIS NEED AN EXCLAMATION POINT?

USE WITH CAUTION

!

"NO WORRIES" | "SOUNDS GOOD"

GREETING | SIGN-OFF

DESCRIPTIVE SUBJECT LINE

IMPORTANT INFORMATION

EMAIL STRUCTURE PYRAMID

September

monday **19**

tuesday **20**

wednesday **21**

thursday **22**

friday **23**   AUTUMN EQUINOX

saturday **24**

NATIONAL PUNCTUATION DAY

sunday **25**

● NEW MOON
ROSH HASHANAH BEGINS

to-dos

HAS THIS*EVER HAPPENED TO YOU?

September/October

monday **26**

tuesday **27**

wednesday **28**

thursday **29**

friday **30**

saturday **1**

BLACK HISTORY MONTH BEGINS (UK, IRL)
GLOBAL DIVERSITY AWARENESS MONTH BEGINS
COFFEE DAY

sunday **2**

to-dos

WILL I EVER USE THE MATH
I LEARNED IN "MEAN GIRLS"?

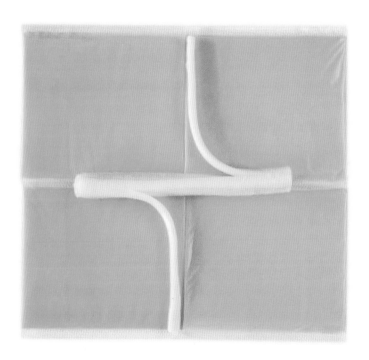

↑ MY CHEESE LIMIT DOES NOT EXIST ↑

October

monday **3** ● FIRST QUARTER
"IT'S OCTOBER THIRD"

tuesday **4** YOM KIPPUR BEGINS

wednesday **5**

thursday **6**

friday **7**

saturday **8**

sunday **9**

○ FULL MOON

to-dos

WHAT SHOULD I DO FOR MY BIRTHDAY?

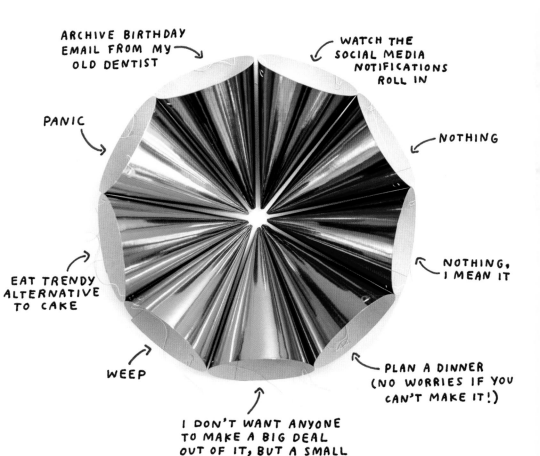

ARCHIVE BIRTHDAY
EMAIL FROM MY
OLD DENTIST

WATCH THE
SOCIAL MEDIA
NOTIFICATIONS
ROLL IN

PANIC

NOTHING

EAT TRENDY
ALTERNATIVE
TO CAKE

NOTHING,
I MEAN IT

WEEP

PLAN A DINNER
(NO WORRIES IF YOU
CAN'T MAKE IT!)

I DON'T WANT ANYONE
TO MAKE A BIG DEAL
OUT OF IT, BUT A SMALL
DEAL WOULD BE NICE

October

monday **10**

INDIGENOUS PEOPLES' DAY (US)
THANKSGIVING (CAN)
WORLD MENTAL HEALTH DAY

tuesday **11**

IT'S MY PARTY DAY

wednesday **12**

thursday **13**

friday **14**

saturday **15**

sunday **16**

to-dos

AM I A BAD FRIEND?

A QUIZ

YOUR FRIEND
GETS GOOD NEWS
(LIKE, *really* GOOD)

↓

HOW DO
YOU FEEL?

IF I'M BEING
HONEST, I FEEL
PRETTY JEALOUS—
IT'S SOMETHING
I'VE WANTED
FOR SO LONG

SOOOOOOO
HAPPY FOR
THEM!!!!

OK, OK

...and?

October

monday **17** ◗ LAST QUARTER

tuesday **18**

wednesday **19** NATIONAL NEW FRIENDS DAY

thursday **20**

friday **21**

saturday **22**

sunday **23**

to-dos

SHOULD I FRAME
THIS MYSELF?

THE WALLS ARE SO EMPTY → I BOUGHT SOME PRINTS

I BOUGHT THE WRONG SIZE FRAMES ← I NEED SOME FRAMES

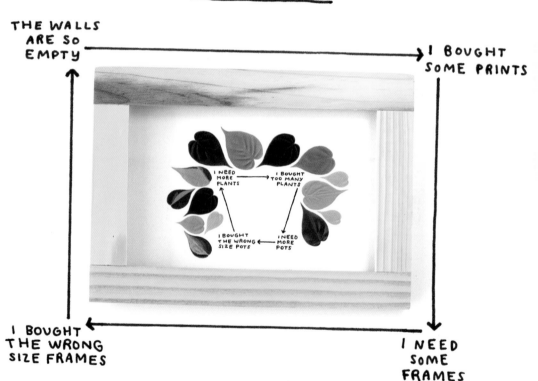

I NEED MORE PLANTS → I BOUGHT TOO MANY PLANTS

I BOUGHT THE WRONG SIZE POTS ← I NEED MORE POTS

October

monday **24**
DIWALI BEGINS
UNITED NATIONS DAY

tuesday **25**
● NEW MOON
NATIONAL ART DAY

wednesday **26**

thursday **27**

friday **28**

saturday **29**

sunday **30**
SUMMER TIME ENDS (UK, IRL)

to-dos
_____
_____
_____
_____
_____
_____
_____
_____
_____
_____
_____
_____
_____
_____
_____
_____
_____
_____
_____
_____
_____
_____
_____
_____

IS IT TOO EARLY TO PLAN MY HALLOWEEN COSTUME?

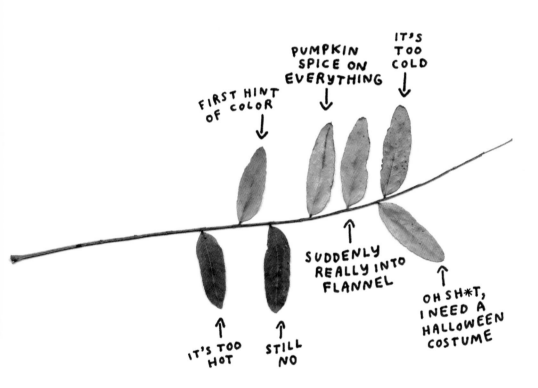

October/November

monday 31
BANK HOLIDAY (IRL)
DÍA DE LOS MUERTOS BEGINS
HALLOWEEN

tuesday 1
◗ FIRST QUARTER

wednesday 2

thursday 3

friday 4

saturday 5
GUY FAWKES NIGHT (UK)

sunday 6
DAYLIGHT SAVING TIME ENDS (US, CAN)

to-dos

WHAT WOULD THE BEATLES DO?

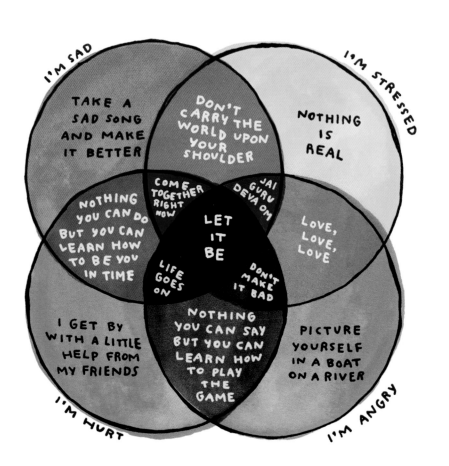

November

monday **7**

tuesday **8**   ○ FULL MOON
ELECTION DAY (US)

wednesday **9**

thursday **10**

friday **11**   VETERANS DAY (US)
REMEMBRANCE DAY (CAN)

saturday **12**

sunday **13**

REMEMBRANCE SUNDAY (UK)
NATIONAL HUG A MUSICIAN DAY

to-dos

SHOULD I GRAB
SOME KALE?

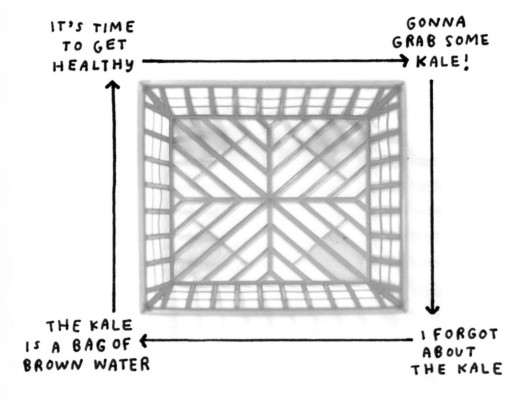

IT'S TIME TO GET HEALTHY

GONNA GRAB SOME KALE!

THE KALE IS A BAG OF BROWN WATER

I FORGOT ABOUT THE KALE

November

monday **14**

tuesday **15**   NATIONAL CLEAN OUT YOUR FRIDGE DAY

wednesday **16**   ◐ LAST QUARTER

thursday **17**

friday **18**

saturday **19**

sunday **20**

to-dos

SHOULD I GIVE MYSELF A BREAK?

WHY AM I
SO HARD ON
MYSELF?

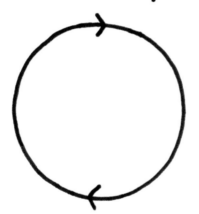

I AM TOO
HARD ON
MYSELF

November

monday **21**	

tuesday **22**	

wednesday **23**	● NEW MOON

thursday **24**	THANKSGIVING (US)

friday **25**	NATIVE AMERICAN HERITAGE DAY (US)

saturday **26**	sunday **27**

to-dos

SHOULD I BUY THIS?

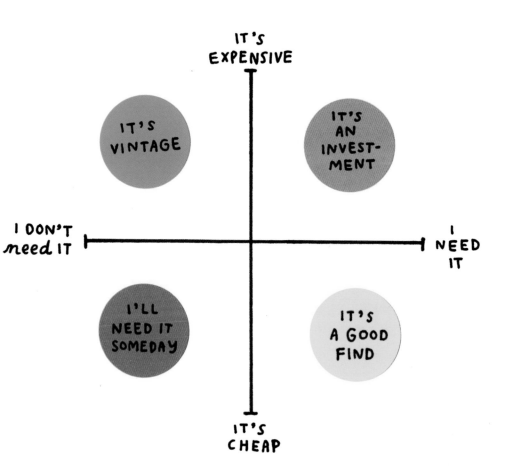

November/December

monday **28** CYBER MONDAY

tuesday **29** GIVING TUESDAY

wednesday **30** ◗ FIRST QUARTER
ST. ANDREW'S DAY (SCT)

thursday **1** WORLD AIDS DAY

friday **2**

saturday **3**
INTERNATIONAL DAY OF DISABLED PERSONS

sunday **4**

to-dos

IS IT WATERMELON SEASON?

SOUTHERN HEMISPHERE

WATERMELON POPULARITY

J F M A M J J A S O N D

MONTH

December

monday **5**

tuesday **6**

wednesday **7**

thursday **8** ○ FULL MOON
NATIONAL BARTENDER DAY

friday **9**

saturday **10**
HUMAN RIGHTS DAY

sunday **11**

to-dos

WHAT IF I FAIL?

	FAILURES	**SUCCESSES**
MANY ATTEMPTS	✚✚✚ ✚✚✚ ✚✚✚ ✚✚✚ ✚✚✚ ✚✚✚ ✚✚✚ ✚✚✚ ✚✚✚ ✚✚✚ ✚✚✚ ✚✚✚	✚✚✚
NO ATTEMPTS	NONE	N/A

December

monday 12

tuesday 13

wednesday 14

thursday 15

friday 16 ☽ LAST QUARTER

saturday 17
NATIONAL RE-GIFTING DAY

sunday 18
CHANUKAH BEGINS

to-dos

EXCITED FOR THE HOLIDAYS?

December

monday 19

tuesday 20

wednesday 21   WINTER SOLSTICE

thursday 22

friday 23 ● NEW MOON

saturday 24

sunday 25

CHRISTMAS

to-dos

HOW DO YOU MEASURE,*
MEASURE A YEAR?

DAYLIGHTS
SUNSETS
MIDNIGHTS
CUPS OF COFFEE
INCHES
MILES
LAUGHTER
STRIFE
525,600 MINUTES
LOVE

LOVE

*ACCORDING TO "RENT"

December/January 2023

monday 26
BOXING DAY
KWANZAA BEGINS
ST. STEPHEN'S DAY (IRL)

tuesday 27
BANK HOLIDAY (UK)

wednesday 28

thursday 29

friday 30 ◗ FIRST QUARTER

saturday 31
NEW YEAR'S EVE

sunday 1
NEW YEAR'S DAY

to-dos

MAYBE WE SHOULD TALK?

MY
BELIEFS

YOUR
BELIEFS

↑

MAYBE YOU CAN
SEE THIS FROM
MY PERSPECTIVE*

* UNLESS ONE OF US IS JUST
REALLY, REALLY WRONG

2021

JANUARY	FEBRUARY	MARCH	APRIL	MAY	JUNE

JANUARY
s m t w t f s
         1 2
3 4 5 6 7 8 9
10 11 12 13 14 15 16
17 18 19 20 21 22 23
24 25 26 27 28 29 30
31

FEBRUARY
s m t w t f s
1 2 3 4 5 6
7 8 9 10 11 12 13
14 15 16 17 18 19 20
21 22 23 24 25 26 27
28

MARCH
s m t w t f s
1 2 3 4 5 6
7 8 9 10 11 12 13
14 15 16 17 18 19 20
21 22 23 24 25 26 27
28 29 30 31

APRIL
s m t w t f s
        1 2 3
4 5 6 7 8 9 10
11 12 13 14 15 16 17
18 19 20 21 22 23 24
25 26 27 28 29 30

MAY
s m t w t f s
           1
2 3 4 5 6 7 8
9 10 11 12 13 14 15
16 17 18 19 20 21 22
23 24 25 26 27 28 29
30 31

JUNE
s m t w t f s
     1 2 3 4 5
6 7 8 9 10 11 12
13 14 15 16 17 18 19
20 21 22 23 24 25 26
27 28 29 30

JULY
s m t w t f s
        1 2 3
4 5 6 7 8 9 10
11 12 13 14 15 16 17
18 19 20 21 22 23 24
25 26 27 28 29 30 31

AUGUST
s m t w t f s
1 2 3 4 5 6 7
8 9 10 11 12 13 14
15 16 17 18 19 20 21
22 23 24 25 26 27 28
29 30 31

SEPTEMBER
s m t w t f s
       1 2 3 4
5 6 7 8 9 10 11
12 13 14 15 16 17 18
19 20 21 22 23 24 25
26 27 28 29 30

OCTOBER
s m t w t f s
         1 2
3 4 5 6 7 8 9
10 11 12 13 14 15 16
17 18 19 20 21 22 23
24 25 26 27 28 29 30
31

NOVEMBER
s m t w t f s
1 2 3 4 5 6
7 8 9 10 11 12 13
14 15 16 17 18 19 20
21 22 23 24 25 26 27
28 29 30

DECEMBER
s m t w t f s
         1 2
5 6 7 8 9 10 11
12 13 14 15 16 17 18
19 20 21 22 23 24 25
26 27 28 29 30 31

2022

JANUARY
s m t w t f s
           1
2 3 4 5 6 7 8
9 10 11 12 13 14 15
16 17 18 19 20 21 22
23 24 25 26 27 28 29
30 31

FEBRUARY
s m t w t f s
    1 2 3 4 5
6 7 8 9 10 11 12
13 14 15 16 17 18 19
20 21 22 23 24 25 26
27 28

MARCH
s m t w t f s
    1 2 3 4 5
6 7 8 9 10 11 12
13 14 15 16 17 18 19
20 21 22 23 24 25 26
27 28 29 30 31

APRIL
s m t w t f s
         1 2
3 4 5 6 7 8 9
10 11 12 13 14 15 16
17 18 19 20 21 22 23
24 25 26 27 28 29 30

MAY
s m t w t f s
1 2 3 4 5 6 7
8 9 10 11 12 13 14
15 16 17 18 19 20 21
22 23 24 25 26 27 28
29 30 31

JUNE
s m t w t f s
         1 2
5 6 7 8 9 10
19 20 21 22 23
26 27 28 29 30

JULY
s m t w t f s
         1 2
3 4 5 6 7 8 9
10 11 12 13 14 15 16
17 18 19 20 21 22 23
24 25 26 27 28 29 30
31

AUGUST
s m t w t f s
1 2 3 4 5 6
7 8 9 10 11 12 13
14 15 16 17 18 19 20
21 22 23 24 25 26 27
28 29 30 31

SEPTEMBER
s m t w t f s
       1 2 3
4 5 6 7 8 9 10
11 12 13 14 15 16 17
18 19 20 21 22 23 24
25 26 27 28 29 30

OCTOBER
s m t w t f s
           1
2 3 4 5 6 7 8
9 10 11 12 13 14 15
16 17 18 19 20 21 22
23 24 25 26 27 28 29
30 31

NOVEMBER
s m t w t f s
1 2 3 4 5
6 7 8 9 10 11 12
13 14 15 16 17 18 19
20 21 22 23 24 25 26
27 28 29 30

DECEMBER
s m t w t f s
           1
4 5 6 7 8
11 12 13 14 15
18 19 20 21 22
25 26 27 28 29

2023

JANUARY
s m t w t f s
1 2 3 4 5 6 7
8 9 10 11 12 13 14
15 16 17 18 19 20 21
22 23 24 25 26 27 28
29 30 31

FEBRUARY
s m t w t f s
       1 2 3 4
5 6 7 8 9 10 11
12 13 14 15 16 17 18
19 20 21 22 23 24 25
26 27 28

MARCH
s m t w t f s
       1 2 3 4
5 6 7 8 9 10 11
12 13 14 15 16 17 18
19 20 21 22 23 24 25
26 27 28 29 30 31

APRIL
s m t w t f s
           1
2 3 4 5 6 7 8
9 10 11 12 13 14 15
16 17 18 19 20 21 22
23 24 25 26 27 28 29
30

MAY
s m t w t f s
   1 2 3 4 5 6
7 8 9 10 11 12 13
14 15 16 17 18 19 20
21 22 23 24 25 26 27
28 29 30 31

JUNE
s m t w t f s
           1
4 5 6 7 8
11 12 13 14 15
18 19 20 21 22
25 26 27 28 29

JULY
s m t w t f s
           1
2 3 4 5 6 7 8
9 10 11 12 13 14 15
16 17 18 19 20 21 22
23 24 25 26 27 28 29
30 31

AUGUST
s m t w t f s
6 7 8 9 10 11 12
13 14 15 16 17 18 19
20 21 22 23 24 25 26
27 28 29 30 31

SEPTEMBER
s m t w t f s
        1 2
3 4 5 6 7 8 9
10 11 12 13 14 15 16
17 18 19 20 21 22 23
24 25 26 27 28 29 30

OCTOBER
s m t w t f s
1 2 3 4 5 6 7
8 9 10 11 12 13 14
15 16 17 18 19 20 21
22 23 24 25 26 27 28
29 30 31

NOVEMBER
s m t w t f s
1 2 3 4
5 6 7 8 9 10 11
12 13 14 15 16 17 18
19 20 21 22 23 24 25
26 27 28 29 30

DECEMBER
s m t w t f s
3 4 5 6 7
10 11 12 13 14
17 18 19 20 21
24 25 26 27 28
31

notes:

notes:

notes:

notes:

notes:

notes:

notes:

notes: